Different kinds of owls live all around the world. They are found on every continent except Antarctica. And they live in many different kinds of places.

Some owls can live in cold climates, and others in warm climates. They may live in dry deserts or rainy jungles. Many owls like wide open spaces, while others stay hidden in the forests.

There are owls living everywhere. So no matter where *you* live, you probably have several different kinds of owls living near you.

CHESTNUT-BACKED OWLET

TUNDRA

SNOWY OWL

This owl lives in the cold, northern *tundra*, where it blends in well with the surroundings. Its long, warm coat of feathers reaches right down to its toes. Even its bill is covered by snowy white feathers.

LONG-EARED OWL

FOREST

opical jungles are home to
ny small owls, like the one at
t. Its small wingspan enables
o fly through the jungle with-
t crashing into trees. And its
autiful red feathers are dark
ough for hiding in the shadows.

BARN OWL

Most owls live in heavily woode
areas. By day, they sleep in tree
where their colors make the
hard to see. At night, many
them, like the Long-eared Owl
left, hunt for mice along th
meadows and roadways near th
edge of the forest.

OPEN FIEL

A white face shaped like a heart
makes this owl easy to recognize.
Barn Owls usually live near farms.
They hunt in open fields. And as you
may have noticed, they have longer
wings than most owls. These are
best for flying over open country
where there are few trees.

ecognizing owls is easy. Just look
a round face, big eyes, and a sharp, hooked
. The face is almost completely covered by
large discs, called *facial discs* (FAY-SHUL
K). Many owls also have feathers sticking
on their heads that look like ears. These
called *ear tufts*.

t is *not* easy to tell one kind of owl from
other. You have to look very carefully. For a
minutes, pretend you are a scientist
dying birds. Look closely at the owls pic-
ed on these pages, but don't read about
m yet. Just see what differences you can
k out.

For example, do the facial discs of some
s look different than others? Do you see
e owls *with* ear tufts, and others *without*?
those with ear tufts all look the same?
at other differences do you see? After you
e studied these owls, read the captions
see how well you did.

GREAT GRAY OWL

EASTERN SCREECH OWL

PEL'S FISHING OWL

Recognizing birds in the wild
is tricky, because you don't
always get a good look at
them. If you saw this owl flying overhead, would you notice its gray color, or the
stripes under its wings?
Would you see the ear tufts,
or the small, oval discs on its
face? If so, you would probably know that this owl is an
Eastern Screech Owl.

Did you notice anything different about
the legs on this owl? They   have
eathers. Fishing Owls d   need
eathers on their legs to protect them
rom their prey. Besides, these feathers
would just get wet and cold.

MALAYSIAN EAGLE OWL

Here's an Eagle Owl
that's easy to recognize.
It has extremely long ear
tufts that stick straight
out on the *sides* of its
head

nese two have very striking faces. heir ear tufts and facial discs line p to make a "V" on their fore- eads. Most Scops Owls have oticeable ear tufts and bushy eathers that cover their beaks like noustaches.

COLLARED SCOPS OWLS

From head to toe, this is a very typical owl. Like many owls, it has ear tufts sticking up on its head. And like most owls, its legs and feet have a thick cover- ing of feathers. This protects them from snakes, rats, and other prey that bites.

Compare this owl's face with the others shown here. Do the other faces look rounder? They should, because Bay Owls and Barn Owls have faces that are shaped like hearts.

BARN OWL

YOUNG TAWNY OWL AND ADULT

Young owls do not look like their parents. For example, *adult* Tawny Owls have red- dish brown feathers, large heads, wide, round facial discs, and big, black eyes. *Young* Tawny Owls have fluffy white feathers. And their eyes are dark blue. Can you tell the young Tawny Owl in this picture from its parent?

An owl's body is ideal for night living. Its superb senses help it to hunt in the dark. For example, owls have the best night vision of any creature on earth. And their hearing is almost as remarkable. An owl can hear the tiny sound of a mouse stepping on a twig from 75 feet away (23 meters).

Owls look the way they do because of these night senses. Their heads have to be large because they have huge eyes and ears. The skull is broad so that both eyes look forward, which makes the owl's vision more accurate. And believe it or not, their facial discs help owls hear better. In these and many other ways, the owl's body is built to make the best possible use of its senses.

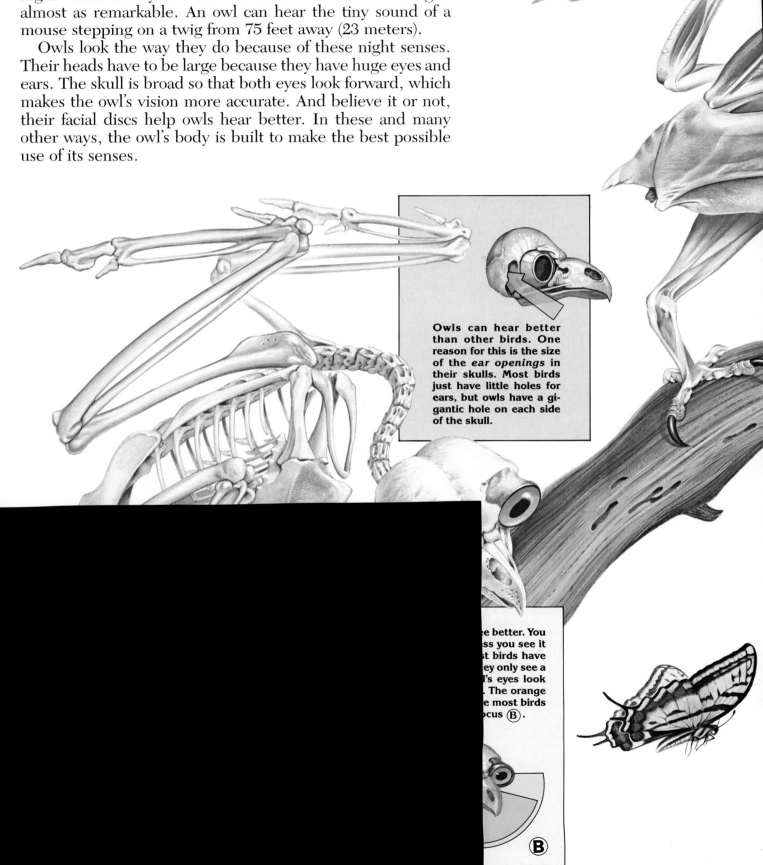

Owls can hear better than other birds. One reason for this is the size of the *ear openings* in their skulls. Most birds just have little holes for ears, but owls have a gigantic hole on each side of the skull.

e better. You
ss you see it
t birds have
ey only see a
l's eyes look
. The orange
e most birds
ocus Ⓑ.

Ⓑ

Most animals that are active at night have big eyes. This allows them to catch almost every bit of light available. But an owl's eyes are so big, they have no room to move up, down, or even sideways.

Because its eyes cannot move, an owl must keep turning its head to follow a moving object. Luckily, its neck is so flexible that it seems to be made of rubber.

An owl can turn its neck so far, and so fast, it sometimes looks as though the head is just spinning like a top!

Imagine that your eyes cannot move, and you can only look straight ahead, like an owl. Your head will only turn far enough to the right and left to let you see what is *in front of you* ①.

An owl can turn its head so far to the right ② that it sees what is behind it. In fact, it can keep turning until it is actually looking over its *left shoulder!* And it can turn its head so far to the left ③ that it ends up looking over the *right shoulder*.

Starting with its head already turned as far as it will go one way, an owl can then turn its head the other way a full circle and a half! ④

Ear tufts aren't ears at all. In fact, owls do not have noticeable ears like ours. They just have big holes hidden behind their facial discs. But these discs work something like our ears. They help funnel sound into the ear openings. An owl can even move its facial discs back and forth slightly, to pick up sounds from different angles.

The wings of most birds have stiff feathers that make noise when they fly Ⓐ. But the feathers on an owl's wing have soft edges Ⓑ, so it can fly more quietly. This way, the owl can listen carefully for its prey, and fly close to it without being heard.

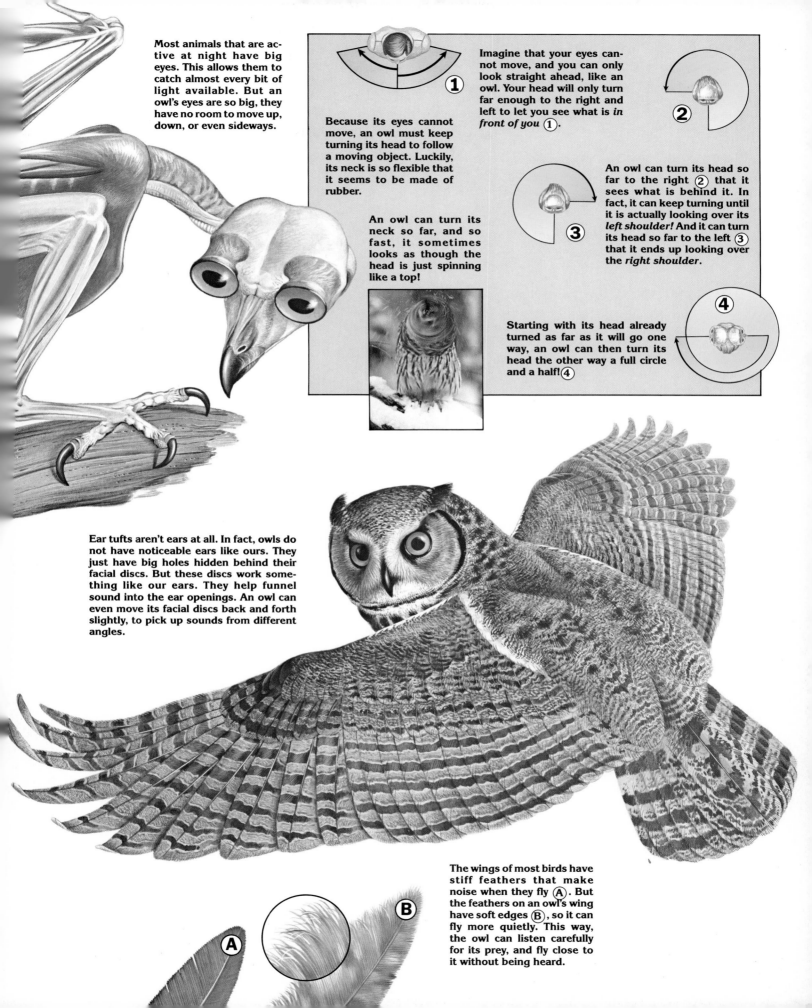

JUVENILE SAW-WHET OWLS

Hunting at night is something that owls do better than any other birds. When hawks and eagles sleep, the owls take over. They hunt in the same areas, and they hunt many of the same kinds of prey. But because of the darkness, owls must use different hunting skills.

When they hunt, owls do not soar like eagles. They do not use long-range vision like hawks. Instead, they fly close to the ground, listening and watching for their prey in the dark.

To hunt, an owl perches silently on a branch. Then it watches and listens for any movement below ①.

An owl's *talons* (TAL-uns), or claws, are dangerous weapons. The way they stab and hold their prey works like the ice hook below, which stabs and holds slippery blocks of ice. Once an animal is in the owl's grasp, it rarely escapes.

When an owl attacks, it spreads all 8 of its toes as far as they'll stretch. This gives the owl a better chance of grabbing its prey in the dark.

SEE FOR YOURSELF why an owl spreads its talons so wide. Place a tiny wad of paper in front of you. Close your eyes and try to touch the paper, using only *one* finger. Now try spreading *all* your fingers as wide as you can. You have a much better chance of striking the paper this way. And that's the way it works for the owl, too.

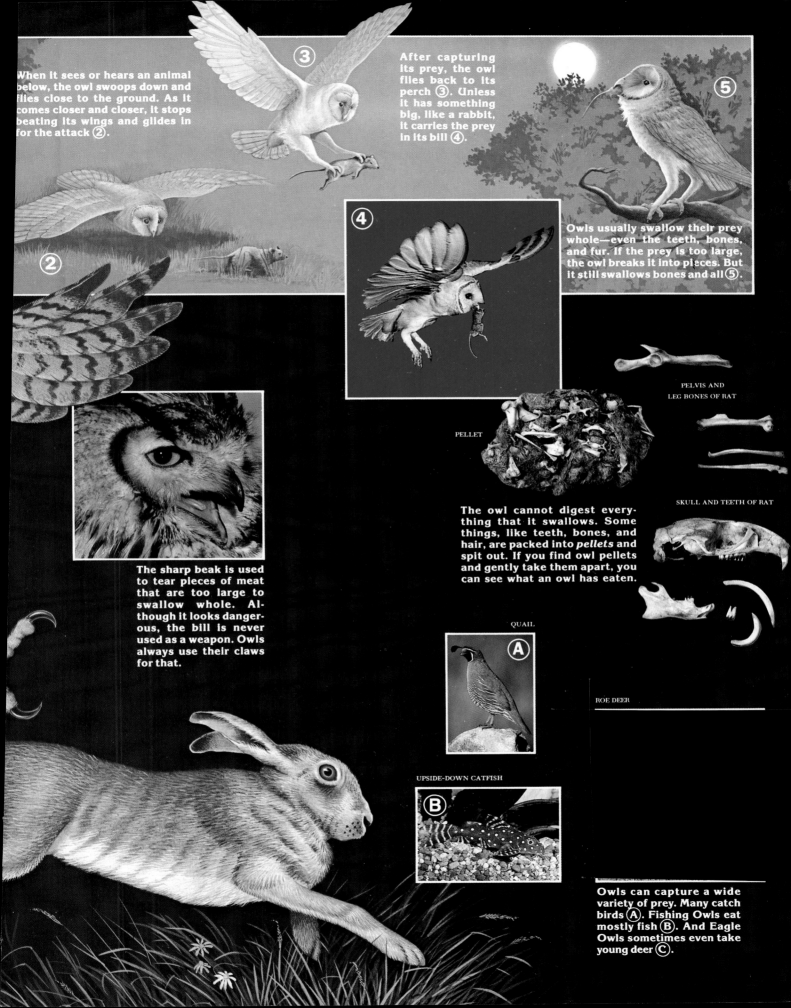

When it sees or hears an animal below, the owl swoops down and flies close to the ground. As it comes closer and closer, it stops beating its wings and glides in for the attack ②.

③

After capturing its prey, the owl flies back to its perch ③. Unless it has something big, like a rabbit, it carries the prey in its bill ④.

⑤

Owls usually swallow their prey whole—even the teeth, bones, and fur. If the prey is too large, the owl breaks it into pieces. But it still swallows bones and all ⑤.

④

PELVIS AND LEG BONES OF RAT

PELLET

The owl cannot digest everything that it swallows. Some things, like teeth, bones, and hair, are packed into *pellets* and spit out. If you find owl pellets and gently take them apart, you can see what an owl has eaten.

SKULL AND TEETH OF RAT

The sharp beak is used to tear pieces of meat that are too large to swallow whole. Although it looks dangerous, the bill is never used as a weapon. Owls always use their claws for that.

QUAIL

Ⓐ

ROE DEER

UPSIDE-DOWN CATFISH

Ⓑ

Owls can capture a wide variety of prey. Many catch birds Ⓐ. Fishing Owls eat mostly fish Ⓑ. And Eagle Owls sometimes even take young deer Ⓒ.

Owls play an important role in nature. Whether we realize it or not, owls affect our lives every day. They help us by controlling rodents and insects.

We tend to forget this, though. And we sometimes even treat owls as our enemies. But they are really the enemies of insects, rodents, and small birds. If it weren't for owls and other predators, the numbers of these animals would zoom out of control.

As it is, owls and their prey are locked in a constant fight for survival. Of course, owls must also compete with each other. And this usually makes them bitter rivals. But as you see in the box at the bottom of the page, some owls solve the problem of competition in a more peaceful way.

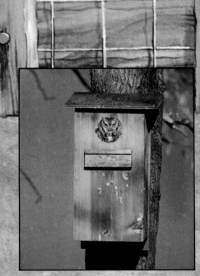

People often chop down old, rotting trees. But this is where many owls like to nest. Luckily, a few people help these owls by building nestboxes where they can live.

GREAT GRAY OWL

Gray Owl is a daytime hunter. Despite its large size, it hunts almost entirely for little rodents called *voles*.

URAL OWL

The Ural Owl can hunt by day or night. But instead of hunting for voles, it usually looks for larger prey, like squirrels.

You may also find a Tawny Owl patrolling the same territory. It hunts voles, but avoids the Great Gray owl by hunting only at night.

TAWNY OWL

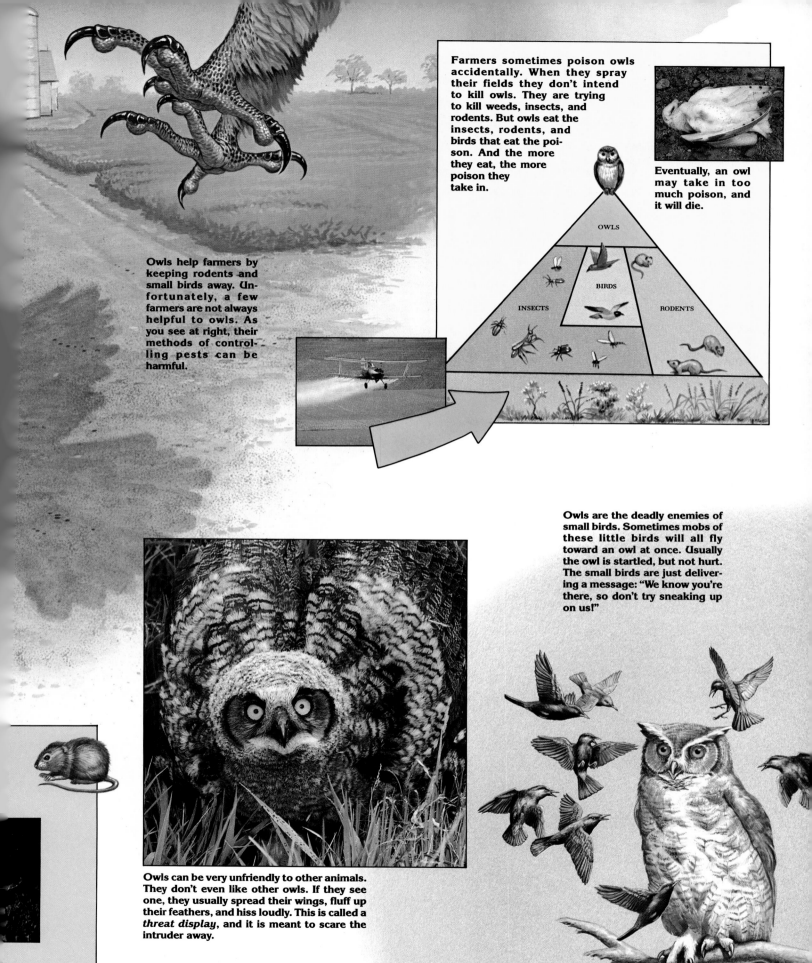

Owls help farmers by keeping rodents and small birds away. Unfortunately, a few farmers are not always helpful to owls. As you see at right, their methods of controlling pests can be harmful.

Farmers sometimes poison owls accidentally. When they spray their fields they don't intend to kill owls. They are trying to kill weeds, insects, and rodents. But owls eat the insects, rodents, and birds that eat the poison. And the more they eat, the more poison they take in.

Eventually, an owl may take in too much poison, and it will die.

OWLS

BIRDS

INSECTS

RODENTS

Owls are the deadly enemies of small birds. Sometimes mobs of these little birds will all fly toward an owl at once. Usually the owl is startled, but not hurt. The small birds are just delivering a message: "We know you're there, so don't try sneaking up on us!"

Owls can be very unfriendly to other animals. They don't even like other owls. If they see one, they usually spread their wings, fluff up their feathers, and hiss loudly. This is called a *threat display*, and it is meant to scare the intruder away.

A mother owl gives her little chicks constant care for almost three months. She feeds them, protects them from danger, and teaches them to fly and hunt. By the time the chicks are three months old, they must be expert hunters. That is when they leave their parents and find territories of their own.

The father owl often helps the mother raise their young. They may find a nest together, and the father may even take his turn sitting on the eggs. After they hatch, he goes hunting and brings back food for the whole family.

Considering how independent adult owls are, it is amazing to see how well mother and father owls can cooperate. But first, they must overcome their natural fear of each other. And this begins as soon as the male courts the female, as you see above.

When he thinks a female is watching him, he lands and drops his prey. With his wings and tail outspread, he struts around the lemming ②.

In the spring, male owls behave in special ways to attract females. For example, the male Snowy Owl carries a lemming in its beak and flies around beating its wings wildly up and down ①.

It takes most young owls about six months before they look like adults. But Spectacled Owls, like those shown below, keep their beautiful white body feathers and dark faces for about *five years*.

The younger brothers and sisters in this family of Spectacled Owls are too young to fly. As with most owl families, there is an age difference of about two days between each of the chicks. Can you tell which of them is the youngest of all?

The number of eggs an owl lays depends on its supply of food. In years when prey is scarce, the owl may lay no eggs at all Ⓐ. If the number of prey is small, it may lay two or three eggs Ⓑ. And in years with plenty of food, there will also be plenty of eggs Ⓒ.

③

If a female approaches him, he turns his back to her and hides the lemming with his wing. He continues to do this while she gradually moves closer. This may go on for hours, but slowly, they begin to lose their fear of each other ③.

YOUNG SCREECH OWLS

BARN OWL CHICKS

Most owls live in trees, but some live in rather unusual places. The family of Screech Owls (above) has moved into an abandoned woodpecker hole in a giant cactus. Barn Owls (top right) often make their homes in the rafters of barns or vacant buildings. And the Burrowing Owl (below right) lives in underground burrows.

BURROWING OWL

This mother Owl is teaching her month-old chicks to fly. With each flight, she increases the distance slightly. And flapping their wings wildly, the chicks try to follow her.

Owls have no fear when it comes to protecting their young. They will swoop down on anything — or anyone — that disturbs their nest. And they strike wildly at the invader with their sharp claws.

Chicks usually hatch two days apart. The oldest chicks grow up to be the strongest, because they get most of the food. When food is scarce, only the oldest chicks get enough to survive. This may seem harsh, but it is nature's way of making sure that at least *some* owls will live.

The future of most owls looks promising—if we are willing to help. People can help owls survive in several ways. The first thing we can do is stop people from poisoning them. We must teach others that poisons are not the *only* way to control rodents and other pests. Unless they are used with extreme caution, these poisons can kill owls, other predators, and maybe even humans.

On the other hand, owls and other predators can help us control pests, if we let them. But they need trees to live in, and land where they can hunt. It is important to leave them enough natural land so they can make their homes and hunt their prey.

That's easier to do for some owls than it is for others. In this century, many of the world's forests have been cleared to make room for cities and farms. This is a problem for Barn Owls, Little Owls, Short-eared Owls, and others that like open spaces. Even many woodland owls, such as the Tawny Owl, the Screech Owl, and the Long-eared Owl, have adjusted well to changes in their habitat.

But other owls have not been so lucky. For example, the Spotted Owl lives in dense evergreen forests and wooded canyons in the western United States. In recent years, people have cleared entire forests to provide lumber for homes and other buildings. This has threatened the survival of the Spotted Owl.

The world's largest owls, the Eurasian Eagle Owls, are also in danger. These owls need large hunting territories and large prey, such as rabbits, ducks and snakes. But they live in heavily populated areas of the world, where these animals are not easy to find.

We can help these and other owls by setting aside wilderness areas where they can live. We can enforce laws that protect owls from being hunted and senselessly killed. And if we must cut down trees, we can put up nestboxes that will make it easier for some owls to live near cities and towns. Working together, we can build a promising future for owls throughout the world.

If you would like to learn how to build a nestbox, write to the following address and ask for "Barn Owl Nestbox Plans":

Soil Conservation Service
332 S. Juniper Street, #110
Escondido, California 92025

ON THE COVER: Eastern Screech Owl

Written by
Timothy Levi Biel

Art Director
Walter Stuart

Creative Administrator
Kelli Leonhardt

Editorial Consultant
John Bonnett Wexo

Zoological Consultant
Charles R. Schroeder, D.V.M.
Director Emeritus
San Diego Zoo &
San Diego Wild Animal Park

Scientific Consultants
Arthur Crane Risser, Ph.D.
Curator of Birds
San Diego Zoo

Kenton C. Lint
Curator of Birds Emeritus
San Diego Zoo

Our Thanks To: Bernard Thornton; Derek Read (British Museum, Tring); Susan Breis; Sarah Feuerstein; Dr. Amadeo Rea (San Diego Museum of Natural History); Ed Hamilton (San Diego Bionomics); Pat Burke (U.S. Soil Conservation Service); Pam Stuart; Andy Lucas.

Printed by World Color; Salem, Illinois

Address Changes: Please include old and new addresses and ZIP codes. Enclose address label from last issue and allow six weeks for change to become effective.

Publisher
Kenneth Kitson

Marketing Director
Gerald E. Marino

Marketing Consultant
Allen Greer

Production
Chris Bateman
Marjorie Shaw
Renee C. Burch
Maurene Mongan

Circulation
Kristine Coryell
Cindy Ostransky
Linda Sambrano
David Bergeman
Shirley Andujo

Accounting
Patricia Krause
Sandra A. Battah
Kymberly Anderson
Kurt Mair

Sales
Kurt Von Hertsenberg
Victoria Selover
Ana Rivera

Administration
Jami Melching
Jill Spencer

June 1992 Volume Nine Number Nine ZOO-BOOKS (ISSN 0737-9005) are published monthly for $15.95 for ten issues by Wildlife Education, Ltd., 3590 Kettner Boulevard, San Diego, California 92101. Second Class postage paid at San Diego, California and additional mailing offices. **POST-MASTER:** Send address changes to ZOOBOOKS, P.O. Box 85384, San Diego, California 92186-5384.

Subscription Rates are $15.95 for 10 issues. Single copy: $2.25 plus $1.50 postage/handling. Send all subscriptions, inquiries and address changes to ZOOBOOKS, P.O. Box 85384, San Diego, California 92186-5384. Telephone (800) 992-5034.

Art Credits
Pages Two and Three: Trevor Boyer; **Pages Six and Seven:** Trevor Boyer; **Page Six: Middle and Bottom,** Walter Stuart; **Page Seven: Upper Right,** Walter Stuart; **Pages Ten and Eleven:** Trevor Boyer; **Page Ten: Bottom Left,** Ed Zilberts; **Page Eleven: Top,** Rebecca Bliss; **Page Twelve:** Walter Stuart; **Page Thirteen: Top,** Walter Stuart; **Bottom,** Rebecca Bliss; **Pages Fourteen and Fifteen: Center,** Trevor Boyer; **Top,** Rebecca Bliss; **Page Fourteen: Bottom,** Raoul Espinoza; **Page Fifteen: Bottom,** Walter Stuart.

Photographic Credits
Front Cover: Robert C. Simpson (Tom Stack and Associates); **Inside Front Cover and Page One:** James R. Fisher (DRK Photo); **Page Two:** Doug Wilson (West Stock); **Page Three: Top Left,** William Boehm (West Stock); **Top Right,** Grant Heilman; **Bottom Right,** Grant Heilman; **Page Four: Top Right,** Pekka Helo (Bruce Coleman, Ltd.); **Middle Left,** Liz & Tony Bomford (Survival Anglia); **Middle Right,** Leonard Lee Rue (Bruce Coleman, Ltd.); **Bottom Right,** C.B. & D.W. Frith (Bruce Coleman, Inc.); **Page Five: Top Left,** Hans Reinhard (Bruce Coleman, Inc.); **Top Middle,** Hans Reinhard (Bruce Coleman, Ltd.); **Top Right,** Ken M. Highfill (Photo Researchers); **Bottom Right,** E. Breeze Jones (Bruce Coleman, Ltd.); **Page Seven:** C.W. Schwartz (Animals Animals); **Pages Eight and Nine:** Rod Planck (Tom Stack and Associates); **Page Ten:** Richard Leonhardt; **Page Eleven: Top Left,** C.F.E. Smedley (Natural Science Photos); **Top Right,** R.J.C. Blewitt (Ardea London); **Middle Left,** Dennis W. Schmidt (Valan Photos); **Middle Right,** Richard Leonhardt; **Bottom Left,** Hans Reinhard (Bruce Coleman, Inc.); **Bottom Right,** Stefan Meyers (Animals Animals); **Page Twelve: Middle,** George H. Harrison (Grant Heilman); **Bottom Left,** Michel Julien (Valan Photos); **Bottom Middle,** Steven Kaufman (Peter Arnold, Inc.); **Bottom Right,** John Daniels (Ardea London); **Page Thirteen: Top,** Em Ahart; **Middle,** Phil Schofield (West Stock); **Bottom,** C.B. Frith (Bruce Coleman, Inc.); **Page Fifteen: Top Left,** C. Allan Morgan; **Top Right,** Alan D. Briere (Tom Stack and Associates); **Middle,** S.L. Craig, Jr. (Bruce Coleman, Inc.); **Bottom,** E. Breeze Jones (Bruce Coleman, Ltd.); **Page Sixteen and Inside Back Cover:** Jeff Foote (Bruce Coleman, Inc.).

Wildlife Education, Ltd. ™

ISBN 0-937934-32-1

T4-AFK-942